First World War
and Army of Occupation
War Diary
France, Belgium and Germany

36 DIVISION
107 Infantry Brigade
Royal Irish Rifles
8/9th Battalion
1 September 1917 - 31 January 1918

WO95/2503/3

The Naval & Military Press Ltd
www.nmarchive.com
Published in association with The National Archives

Published by

The Naval & Military Press Ltd

Unit 10 Ridgewood Industrial Park,

Uckfield, East Sussex,

TN22 5QE England

Tel: +44 (0) 1825 749494

www.naval-military-press.com

www.nmarchive.com

This diary has been reprinted in facsimile from the original. Any imperfections are inevitably reproduced and the quality may fall short of modern type and cartographic standards.

© Crown Copyright
Images reproduced by permission of The National Archives, London, England, 2015.

Contents

Document type	Place/Title	Date From	Date To
Heading	WO95/2503/3 8/9 Battalion Royal Irish Rifles		
Heading	36th Division 107 Inf Bde 8/9 Bn R Irish Rifles 1917 Sept-1918 Jan		
War Diary	Equancourt	01/09/1917	30/09/1917
War Diary	Ref. Sheet 57.S E. 1/20,000 Trenches	01/10/1917	03/10/1917
War Diary	Metz	04/10/1917	09/10/1917
War Diary	Trenches	10/10/1917	15/10/1917
War Diary	Equancourt	16/10/1917	21/10/1917
War Diary	Trenches	22/10/1917	27/10/1917
War Diary	Metz	28/10/1917	31/10/1917
War Diary	Reference Sheet 57c. 1/40,0000. 57 C N.E. 1/20,000 Metz	01/11/1917	01/11/1917
War Diary	Trenches	02/11/1917	07/11/1917
War Diary	Ytres	07/11/1917	12/11/1917
War Diary	Trenches	13/11/1917	18/11/1917
War Diary	Lechelle	19/11/1917	20/11/1917
War Diary	Havrincourt	21/11/1917	21/11/1917
War Diary	Trenches	22/11/1917	26/11/1917
War Diary	Hermies	27/11/1917	27/11/1917
War Diary	Barastre	28/11/1917	28/11/1917
War Diary	Berneville	29/11/1917	30/11/1917
War Diary	Ref Lens 11 1/100.000 Courcelles-Le-Comte	01/12/1917	02/12/1917
War Diary	Lechelle	03/12/1917	04/12/1917
War Diary	Trenches	05/12/1917	06/12/1917
War Diary	Metz	07/12/1917	08/12/1917
War Diary	Trenches	09/12/1917	14/12/1917
War Diary	Metz	15/12/1917	15/12/1917
War Diary	Etricourt	16/12/1917	17/12/1917
War Diary	Ivergny	18/12/1917	27/12/1917
War Diary	Blangy	28/12/1917	31/12/1917
War Diary	Blangy Tronville	01/01/1918	07/01/1918
War Diary	Rosieres	08/01/1918	10/01/1918
War Diary	Voyennes	11/01/1918	11/01/1918
War Diary	Douchy	12/01/1918	16/01/1918
War Diary	Grugies	17/01/1918	31/01/1918

WO95/2503/3
8/9 Battalion Royal Irish Rifles

36 DIVISION

107 INF BDE

8/9 BN R IRISH RIFLES

1917 SEPT — 1918 JAN

DISBANDED

WAR DIARY or INTELLIGENCE SUMMARY.

(Erase heading not required.)

Army Form C. 2118.

Place	Date	Hour	Summary of Events and Information	Remarks and references to Appendices
EQUANCOURT	1.9.17		Battalion in billets at EQUANCOURT. 1 Company on Parade. 3 Companies on working parties at Front Line and Supports.	
"	2.9.17		Interior economy during morning. In the afternoon the Battalion proceeded by train to HAVRINCOURT trenches WOOD and from there proceeded by route march to the trenches on the HAVRINCOURT Sector, relieving the 15th Bn. Royal Irish Rifles on the line.	
	3.9.17 to 8.9.17		Battalion in the trenches, very quiet time during the tour. 1 O.R. slightly wounded.	
	8.9.17		Battalion relieved in the line by the 15th Bn Royal Irish Rifles. After relief the Battalion withdrew to billets in METZ and were in Brigade Reserve.	
	9.9.17 to 10.9.17		Battalion in billets at METZ. Day devoted to Interior economy and found working parties for the line – 5 Officers 18,359 O.R.	
	11.9.17		G.O.C. IV Corps inspected the Battalion at METZ, a very good inspection and parade. The B.C.O. IV Corps spoke very highly of the Battalion, after the inspection the Battalion marched past on fours.	
	12.9.17		Working parties found for the line etc. 5 Officers and 340 O.R.	
	13.9.17		Day devoted to Brigade under Company arrangements Battalion Parade (Alpaards) 9.30 a.m. to 10.30 a.m.	
	14.9.17		Interior economy during the morning. In the afternoon the Battalion moved up to the line. HAVRINCOURT Sector and relieved the 15th Bn Royal Irish Rifles. A good relief	

Army Form C. 2118.

WAR DIARY
or
INTELLIGENCE SUMMARY.
(Erase heading not required.)

Instructions regarding War Diaries and Intelligence
Summaries are contained in F. S. Regs., Part II.
and the Staff Manual respectively. Title pages
will be prepared in manuscript.

Place	Date	Hour	Summary of Events and Information	Remarks and references to Appendices
	16.9.17 to 20.9.17		Battalion in the trenches, a very good time. 1. O.R. killed 2 wounded.	
	21.9.17		Battalion relieved in the line by the 15th Bn Royal Irish Rifles. Good relief. After which the Battalion withdrew to billets at EQUANCOURT and was in Divisional Reserve. Battalion marched to HAVRINCOURT WOOD, and these entrained detraining at EQUANCOURT.	
	22.9.17 23.9.17 24.9.17		Battalion in billets at EQUANCOURT. Day devoted to Interior economy. Parades under Company arrangements. " " " " " " " " G.O.C. 36th Division carried out inspection of Battalion. Transport and Battalion Billets. Highly successful. Parades under Company arrangements.	
	25.9.17 26.9.17		" " " " " " Parades under Company arrangements.	
	27.9.17		Battalion parade in the morning. In the afternoon the Battalion proceeded by rail to HAVRINCOURT WOOD and thence by march route to the trenches and relieved 15th Bn Royal Irish Rifles. Relief complete 6 p.m.	
	28.9.17 to 30.9.17		Battalion in trenches. Very quiet time, 2 O.R. killed and 3 O.R. wounded.	

H.C. Rupe & Lieut. Colonel.
Commanding 8/9th Bn Royal Irish Rifles.
1st October 1917.

WAR DIARY

INTELLIGENCE SUMMARY

9th Ser. Bn. Roy. Irish Rifles.

Army Form C. 2118.

October 1917

Place	Date	Hour	Summary of Events and Information	Remarks and references to Appendices
Ref. Sheet 57cS.E. 1/20,000 TRENCHES	1/10/17		Battalion in trenches. Cwal. Times. Casualties nil.	
do	2/10/17		— do — — do —	
do	3/10/17		Relieved by 15th Bn. Royal Irish Rifles and withdrew into Brigade Reserve at METZ.	
METZ	4/10/17		Spent in interior economy under Coy arrangements	
do	5/10/17		Battalion on working parties. The following rewards for services in the field were announced — The Military Cross to 2/Lieut (a/Capt) J. IRELAND. Bar to the Military Medal — No. 8/11151 2/Lieut (a/Corpl) D. McMULLAN. Military Medal — No. 3/9352 Corpl D. MORTON, No. 8/13798 Rfn A.W. WRIGHT, No. 6/11421 Rfn J. McLAUGHLIN, No. 8/13873 Rfn H. WILSON and No. 9/15363 L/Cpl S. McGLINTON	
do	6/10/17		Battalion on working parties. Church parade for men not working.	

H.S. Weir
Lieut. Colonel,
Commdg. 9th Bn. Royal Irish Rifles.

WAR DIARY
INTELLIGENCE SUMMARY.
(Erase heading not required.)

9th Ser. Bn. Roy. Irish Rifles.   October 1917.   Army Form C. 2118.

Instructions regarding War Diaries and Intelligence Summaries are contained in F. S. Regs., Part II. and the Staff Manual respectively. Title pages will be prepared in manuscript.

Place	Date	Hour	Summary of Events and Information	Remarks and references to Appendices
M.F.2.	oct. 1917		Battalion on working parties	
do	9		The Battalion relieved the 15th Bn Roy. Ir. Rifles in the trenches (TRESCAUNT Right Sub Sector). Quiet relief. Capt. & Adjt. A.E.C. THORNTON proceeded to the United Kingdom for 6 months duty. Capt. J.C. DOUGLAS assumed duties of Adjutant.	
Trenches	10-14		Battalion in trenches. Quiet time.	
do	15		Battalion relieved by 15th Bn Royal Irish Rifles & withdrew into Divisional Reserve at EQUANCOURT by light Railway. Casualties during tour — 3 o.r. wounded.	
EQUANCOURT	16		Intensive economy under Coy arrangements.	
do	17/18		Training programme carried out under Coy Commanders. Football match played on 17/10/17 with D.R.C. — Result 9/R.I.R. b goals D.R.C. nil. Lieut. W.L. FRYHT reported for duty.	
do	19		Training carried out.	
			and assumed duties of Batn. Lewis Gun Officer. Football match played on 19.10.17 with 9th R.I.R. v goals 9/R.I.R. two nil	
do	20		Battalion carried out training.	
do	21		Church parades on morning. In afternoon proceeded to the trenches (Trescault Right Sub Sector) by Light Railway and relieved	

Lieut. Colonel,
Commdg/9th Bn. Royal Irish Rifles.

WAR DIARY

/9th Ser. Bn. Roy. Irish Rifles.

October 1917

Army Form C. 2118.

INTELLIGENCE SUMMARY

Place	Date	Hour	Summary of Events and Information	Remarks and references to Appendices
EQUANCOURT Trenches	Oct 25		The 15th Bn. Royal Irish Rifles Battalion in trenches.	
do.	26		The following promotions appeared in London Gazette of 17 Nov. 3/Lt. to be Temp Lts. – P.R.G. Abernethy, R. Baillie, J.H. Witherow, W. Wilson, V. Unsworth, M.P. (all 1st July 1917) R.E. Pattison, S.A. Lynch, (6th July 1917) D.R. Bates (8th July 1917) 2/Lts R.K. Knox, R. Young and W.H. McNeill reported from arrival and were posted to C,B & D Coys respectively.	
do.	27		Battalion was relieved by the 15th Bn. Roy. I.F. Rifles and withdrew to Brigade Reserves in METZ. Casualties during tour – 2 O.R. killed 5 O.R. wounded.	
METZ	28			
do.	29/1		Church parades and interior economy under Coy arrangements. Football match with 1st R.I.R. 9.30 in aftnoon which the Coys played. Result 9th R.I.R. 1 goal, 1st R.I.R. 1 goal Nil. Battalion on working parties.	

Lieut. Colonel,
Commdg. 9th Bn. Royal Irish Rifles.

8/9 th Bn. Royal Irish Rifles.

WAR DIARY

November 1917.

Army Form C. 2118.

Place	Date	Hour	Summary of Events and Information	Remarks and references to Appendices
Reference Sheet.		57C. N.W. 1/40,000 57C. S.W. 1/20,000		
METZ.	1-11-17		Battalion in METZ. Working parties in morning. Afternoon spent in interior economy.	
Trenches.	2-11-17		Moved into trenches at 1.45 p.m. and relieved 15th Bn. Royal Irish Rifles, the TRESGAULT Right Sub-Sector. Fairly quick relief. 2nd Lt. E. HUTCHINSON was transferred to England to Commission Indian N.A. & Struck off strength. Battalion in trenches. Very quiet. Timely.	
"	3-11-17 to 6-11-17		2nd Lieut. L.S. KIDD joined for duty 6-11-17 and was taken on strength in the trenches. 2nd Lieut. J. CRESWELL was transferred to England, sick 3-11-17 and struck off strength.	
"	7-11-17		Were relieved in the line by the 15th Bn. Royal Irish Rifles, and withdrew to camp at VAULX & WOOD. (P.26. d.8.1.) by march route. Arrived in Camp 8 p.m.	
YTRES.	7-11-17 to 12-11-17		Monotonous time at YTRES. Men all engaged in working parties loading & unloading ammunition at YTRES Railway Station. 2nd Lieuts. M.F. LANE joined for duty 13-11-17 & 2nd Lt. J.A. STEVENSON 9-11-17 and both were taken on strength.	
Trenches.	13-11-17		Moved by march route and relieved 15th Bn. Royal Irish Rifles in TRESGAULT Right Sub-Sector.	
"	14-11-17		Enemy showed slightly more activity. Very busy preparing line for offensive operations and showing various Officers and N.C.O's round the line.	
"	18-11-17		Relieved in trenches by parts of 152nd and 153rd Inf. Brigades. Two Companies relieved by 9.30 a.m and remaining two by 7.30 p.m. On relief withdrew to LECHELLE and spent rest of day issuing Battle Equipment and preparing for offensive.	
LECHELLE	19-11-17		Moved from LECHELLE to field at J.34.C. arriving at 8.40 a.m. Ammunition and Bombs were issued and Battalion reported ready to move at 9.30 a.m. and remained in the open in J.5.d. & 31.b. at 1.40 p.m. when orders were received to move to HAVRINGCOURT CANAL	
"	20-11-17	6.15a.m 1.40 p.m	Moved to fill in J.25.d. & 31.b. at 1.40 p.m when orders were received to move to HAVRINGCOURT CANAL. Gentle rain until 9.30 p.m. Canal was crossed by a single foot bridge, and consequently progress was very slow, but HAVRINGCOURT was reached about 7.30 a.m/21/8 and remainder of night was spent under any cover available.	

J.P. Ussher Lieut-Col
Commanding 8/9 th Bn Royal Irish Rifles

WAR DIARY / INTELLIGENCE SUMMARY

8/9th Bn. Royal Irish Rifles. November, 1917. Army Form C. 2118.

Place	Date	Hour	Summary of Events and Information	Remarks and references to Appendices
HAVRINCOURT.	21-11-17		On the arrival of daylight, more or less comfortable billets were found for all ranks and the Battalion stood by, waiting for orders to move. These were received at 3.45 p.m. and the Battalion moved to HINDENBURG SUPPORT Line in K.10.D. Arrived about 7.15 p.m. and got more or less comfortably established in trenches and dug-outs. Battalion Headquarters in 105 m.m. Gun pit at K.10.K.1.8.	
Trenches.	22-11-17		At about 9.30 a.m. Orders were received to man KANGAROO ALLEY immediately as the enemy was counter attacking. This was done; Headquarters first being established at K.4.d.1.5. and later at K.4.a.30.05. Remainder of day passed uneventfully.	
"	23-11-17		Early in morning Orders received for attack as follows:— At 10.30 a.m., two platoons B Coy were to attack Lock 5; 1 platoon B Coy and 1 platoon D Coy were to attack ROUND TRENCH in co-operation with 10th and 15th Bns. Royal Irish Rifles on right attacking HINDENBURG SUPPORT Line as far as CANAL at 6.15.c.3.1. Remainder of the Battalion being previously moved to trenches North of CAMBRAI-BAPAUME Road. was to move up to assembly positions in HINDENBURG SUPPORT from 6.21.6.1.6. to 6.22.6.0.3. and at 1 p.m. was to attack and consolidate QUARRY WOOD (6.10.a.) in co-operation with 1st Bn. Royal Irish Fusiliers attacking on left. / In the attack at 10.30 a.m. the Battalion took both objectives, but the 10th and 15th Bns R.I. Rifles failed and the rest of the Battalion moving up to assemble in the HINDENBURG SUPPORT Line came under concentrated Machine Gun fire and were unable to get further forward than a line 6.21.6.2.2. to 6.22.a.8.1. where they had to lie down in the open. / At 4.35 p.m. Orders received to withdraw to trench North of CAMBRAI-BAPAUME ROAD. Lock No.5 and ROUND TRENCH to be held. This was immediately done and at 7 p.m. "B" Company were withdrawn to CAMBRAI - BAPAUME Road. Headquarters established at 6.27.D.4.7.	

V.R. Ellis Lieut-Col.
Commanding 8/9th Bn. Royal Irish Rifles.

8/9th Bn. Royal Irish Rifles.   November, 1917.   Army Form C. 2118.

WAR DIARY or INTELLIGENCE SUMMARY

(Erase heading not required.)

Instructions regarding War Diaries and Intelligence Summaries are contained in F.S. Regs. Part II. and the Staff Manual respectively. Title pages will be prepared in manuscript.

Place	Date	Hour	Summary of Events and Information	Remarks and references to Appendices
Trenches.	24-11-17	10.30 a.m.	Location of Battalion at 10.30 a.m. Battalion Headquarters C.27.d.4.7. One platoon B. Company, Round Trench. Two platoons C. Coy. Loch 165. B. Coy. D. Coy less 1 platoon, C. Coy less 1 platoon in trench N. of CAMBRAI-BAPAUME Road from HINDENBURG SUPPORT Line to the CANAL. B. Coy on CAMBRAI-BAPAUME Road. Day passed quietly. 1st Bn. Royal Irish Fusiliers attempted to take the HINDENBURG SUPPORT Line but failed.	"J.P." Wars Lieut-Col. Commanding 8/9th Bn. Royal Irish Rifles.
"	25-11-17		Acting on Brigade Instructions B. Company all moved forward to the trench N. of CAMBRAI-BAPAUME Road. Day spent in consolidation.	
"	26-11-17		In afternoon Locks and trench N. of CAMBRAI-BAPAUME Road as far as SUNKEN ROAD. C.27.d.4.3. were relieved by 9th Bn. Royal Inniskilling Fusiliers and commencing at 11 p.m. the remaining 2 companies were relieved by the 22nd Bn. Royal Fusiliers and the Battalion withdrew to HERMIES. Relief complete 1.30 a.m. Casualties during operations:- Officers killed, 2nd Lieut C.V. BOYD and 2nd Lieut J. SMITH. Wounded, Lieut J.W. MILLIGAN, 2nd Lieut H.B. MITCHELL + 2nd Lieut J. SOMERSET (at duty), 16 ORks killed, 151 ORks wounded, and 10 ORks missing.	
HERMIES.	27-11-17		Battalion moved to hutted camp at BARASTRE in afternoon, where details left out of action rejoined.	
BARASTRE	28-11-17		Spent in re-organisation.	
BERNEVILLE.	29-11-17		Marched to YTRES and entrained; detrained RIVIERE and marched to BERNEVILLE. Arrived 3-30 p.m.	
"	30-11-17	12.30 p.m.	At 12.30 p.m. Orders received to prepare to move at once and at 2-30 p.m. the Battalion moved off by March Route to COURCELLES-LE-COMTE, arriving 8-30 p.m.	

December 1917.

WAR DIARY
INTELLIGENCE SUMMARY.
(Erase heading not required.)

Army Form C.2118.

Place	Date	Hour	Summary of Events and Information	Remarks and references to Appendices
	December			
COURCELLES-LE-COMTE.	1.		Marched to BEAULENCOURT in afternoon & arrived about 8 P.M. Bivouacked in NISSEN Huts.	
	2.		Continued march to LECHELLE, starting at about 10 A.M. Accommodated in Hutted camp. 2/Lieuts C.P. Seath & W.J. Davies joined.	
LECHELLE	3.		Stood by waiting for orders. Advantage was taken of the halt to re-organise Companies & prepare for Battle	
"	4.		Moved about mid-day up to the line 9 Coyto aux LINCOLN AVENUE trenches near VILLERS PLOUICH (Front Sheet 57c S.E - R13) at dusk. Relief left out Garrison went to MANANCOURT.	
Trenches	5.		Held line, everything quite quiet.	
"	6.		Withdrew to METZ at dusk.	
METZ	7.		Interior economy and drill.	
"	8.		Relieved 10" R. Innis. Fus in left Sub-section, holding from grid-line between R40 R10 to R5a 0.3.	
Trenches	9.		Battn. moved from MANANCOURT - SOREL-LE-GRAND. Battalion remained in line.	
"	10-13.		Remained in line. No operations developed on either side & everything quite quiet. Trench conditions rather bad. Casualties light.	

Army Form C. 2118.

WAR DIARY
or
INTELLIGENCE SUMMARY.
(Erase heading not required.)

Instructions regarding War Diaries and Intelligence Summaries are contained in F.S. Regs., Part II. and the Staff Manual respectively. Title pages will be prepared in manuscript.

Place	Date	Hour	Summary of Events and Information	Remarks and references to Appendices
Trenches	14		Relieved at night by HAWKE Battalion. Fairly quick relief. On completion of relief returned to METZ.	
METZ.	15		Marched to ETRICOURT in afternoon where details rejoined. Accomodated in huts pitched on top of a hill.	
ETRICOURT	16		Bitterly cold day. Church Parade 9 a.m. Baths & a rum ration occupied the day. In evening commenced to snow.	Major Bromby s/s Bn. Leg Inertshire
	17		Moved off at 9 A.M., entrained 10.30 A.M. at ETRICOURT STATION, march by train to MONDICOURT where Battn detrained at 3.45 P.M. Ground deep in snow & very cold journey. Marched via LUCHEUX to IVERGNY where we billeted. Arrived at about 7 P.M.	Grimsworth
IVERGNY	18/26		Remained at IVERGNY, billets quite comfortable but rather cold. Worked on the mods, cleaning the of arms & leaving economy the Battalion was billeted at GRAND ROLLECOURT on 24 & 25. Portion of the transport moved off by Road to the CORBIE area on the 26" staging at PUCHEVILLERS on the night 26/27A.	
	27.		Battalion marched off at 5.O.A.M. & marched to MONDICOURT where by it entrained & travelled to CORBIE where it detrained & marched to AUBIGNY. From	

A6945 Wt. W14422/M160 350,000 12/16 D.D. & L. Forms/C/2118/14.

Army Form C. 2118.

WAR DIARY
INTELLIGENCE SUMMARY.
(Erase heading not required.)

Instructions regarding War Diaries and Intelligence Summaries are contained in F. S. Regs., Part II. and the Staff Manual respectively. Title pages will be prepared in manuscript.

Place	Date	Hour	Summary of Events and Information	Remarks and references to Appendices
BLANGY	28.		Here the march was continued by Companies, O Coy going to LAMOTTE, C Coy to GUISY, A & B Coy to BLANGY- FROMVILLE & Hd-Qrs to TRAMVILLE CHATEAU. Arrived about 7 P.M. and found billets very comfortable.	
"	29-31		"D" Coy moved from LAMOTTE to GUISY. Training programme was carried out.	

8/9th Royal Irish Rifles. January 1918. Army Form C. 2118.

WAR DIARY
of
INTELLIGENCE SUMMARY.
(Erase heading not required.)

Instructions regarding War Diaries and Intelligence Summaries are contained in F.S. Regs. Part II. and the Staff Manual respectively. Title pages will be prepared in manuscript.

Place	Date	Hour	Summary of Events and Information	Remarks and references to Appendices
BLANGY TRONVILLE.	1.1.18 to 6.1.18		The Battalion in CORBIE Area. Weather very cold. Work carried out on the Roads clearing snow. Half the Battalion in training.	
"	7.1.18		The Battalion moved by march route to ROSIÈRES via VILLERS - BRETTONEUX - LA MOTTE BAYONVILLERS - HARBONNIERS.	
ROSIERES.	8.1.18 to 10.1.18		The Battalion moved by march route to VOYENNES. Route via LIHONS - CHAULNES - PUZEAUX - NESLE - Arrived 15 C. in Corpt MANCHE.	
VOYENNES	11.1.18		The Battalion moved by march route to AUBIGNY. Route via MATIGNY - ST SULPICE.	
DOUCHY.	12.1.18 to 16.1.18		The Battalion relieved the 3rd Batt. 24th French Infantry Regiment on the Right Sub-Sector. Very quiet time.	
GRUGIES	17.1.18 to 23.1.18		The Battalion relieved in the Front Line by the 15th Bn Royal Irish Rifles on the night of the 18/19th. Good relief. After relief the Battalion withdrew to the Support Battalion Area. Found Working parties for Front Line.	
"	23.1.18 to 28.1.18		The Battalion relieved the 15th Bn Royal Irish Rifles in Front Line. Very quiet time.	
"	29.1.18 to 31.1.18		The Battalion relieved by the 15th Batt. Royal Irish Rifles in the Front Line on the night 30/31st. After relief the Battalion withdrew into Brigade Support.	
"			The Battalion in Brigade Support.	

www.ingramcontent.com/pod-product-compliance
Lightning Source LLC
Chambersburg PA
CBHW081253170426
43191CB00037B/2139